AJAR

POEMS

ESSENTIAL POETS SERIES 319

Canada

Guernica Editions Inc. acknowledges the support of
the Canada Council for the Arts and the Ontario Arts Council.
The Ontario Arts Council is an agency of the Government of Ontario.

We acknowledge the financial support of the Government of Canada.

MARGO LAPIERRE

AJAR

POEMS

GUERNICA
EDITIONS

TORONTO • CHICAGO
BUFFALO • LANCASTER (U.K.)
2025

Guernica founder: Antonio D'Alfonso

Michael Mirolla, editor
Cover and interior design: Rafael Chimicatti
Front cover art: Nithya Swaminathan

Guernica Editions Inc.
1241 Marble Rock Rd., Gananoque, (ON), Canada K7G 2V4
2250 Military Road, Tonawanda, N.Y. 14150-6000 U.S.A.
www.guernicaeditions.com

Distributors:
University of Toronto Press Distribution (UTP)
5201 Dufferin Street, Toronto (ON), Canada M3H 5T8
Independent Publishers Group (IPG)
814 N Franklin Street, Chicago, IL 60610, U.S.A.

First edition.
Printed in Canada.

Legal Deposit – Third Quarter
Library of Congress Catalogue Card Number: 2025934906
Library and Archives Canada Cataloguing in Publication
Title: Ajar : poems / Margo LaPierre.
Names: LaPierre, Margo, author.
Series: Essential poets ; 319.
Description: Series statement: Essential poets series ; 319
Identifiers: Canadiana 20250169908 | ISBN 9781771839884 (softcover)
Subjects: LCGFT: Poetry.
Classification: LCC PS8623.A7253 A78 2025 | DDC C811/.6—dc23

CONTENTS

Inviolate

Close your eyes next to me.
A symphony layers years upon our bodies.
A rising cello note, and we hover
like breath.
Your name is a hand I want to hold.
My name is lily of the valley,
delicate and filled with poison,
early to bloom in the shadowed paths
behind the apartment, where robin nestlings drop
to independence, mauve sealed eyes
like capers and roe,
that is my name—
a thing to be snuffed.

Cento for Psychometry

Do you feel the chill of time? It's a frozen plum.
Losing. What would I be losing if I left.
In my doorway. In my nakedness, let me explain.

Anna Van Valkenburg, "A Frozen Plum Tells Time" / Roxanna Bennett, "Waiting List" / Shira Erlichman, "Ghazal, Interrupted"

The Grapefruit: Assembly

The snow recedes in the yard, revealing chives,
leaf litter, daylilies I wish were tulips,
broken chairs, a gaping dresser,
my upstairs neighbour's wet books, stuck in the ice.

In utero, nightmares grew in me. It's morning now.
I write them down, go to the screen door, check the weather,
choose clothing and a grapefruit that I cut in half
and eat. I read a book of poetry.

Time is no longer an emergency. The clock deciduous,
moulting its hands like spring down.

Bang and zest. Let's rewind. Where was I?
Domestic objects? Oh, yes. Bad dreams.

When my name was dropped on my head in spotted sun-
shine, I mistook real for unreal and I haunted me.

When I saw forward into my death and welcomed
its yawn, I haunted me.

Each time as a child I refused to play the Ouija board,
it was to make sure nothing haunted me but me.

The Grapefruit: Noon

I slide my hands along my hipbones,
down the bedside glass of water with my pill.
The robin sprints the lawn for a worm.

In the closet, my long cotton dress
and comfy sweater. I lay them on the bed,
stomp flat-foot heel-first into the kitchen.

Can't talk to stone about a poem.
I'd try, but there's a word for that, a higher dose.
My head already a gauzy white corsage.

Amethysts & Satellites: On Categorization of Phenomena in Psychosis

Rain. Do you hear the radio? No—just me?
        The screen door doesn't close properly.

I'm unsure if the strain is a low satellite passing
        or the maw of my sanity.

Low, flat, gurgling, alien—it drones
        over rooftops
        beyond a drafty south-facing screen,
        where cranes erecting towers mine
        amethysts from the cloud cover.
        Rain. Let us have it.

Rain. The pigment brazen
on the cloud bank's underbelly.

Quinacridone is an odd name
for backyard raspberries.
Mix it with ultramarine
and you get the heavy part
        of buoyancy.

What's that? More rain?
Organized static, singing.
Advice splinters into puddles,
the sky sits in her rain,
bellowing orange.

If it *is* a low satellite, sending messages,
there will be a sound
        like a package arriving.

The Grapefruit: A Model of Time Squeezed through Consciousness

Our pasts and futures chirp at midnight.
With trauma or in psychosis, time flattens—or we do.
Consider the zipper model from the perspective
of your death, that dotted line a dusty grid. You'll see
a halved grapefruit pressed against a screen door.

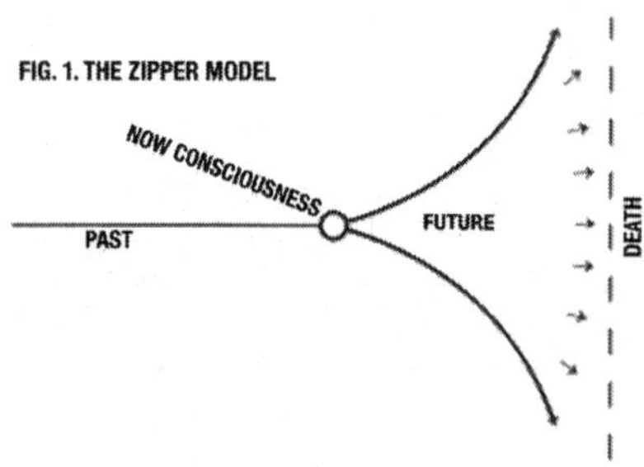

FIG. 1. THE ZIPPER MODEL

FIG. 2. HALVED GRAPEFRUIT PRESSED AGAINST A SCREEN DOOR

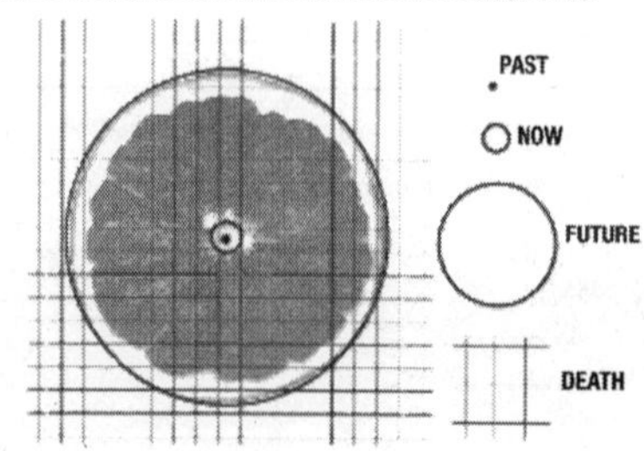

Causation travels backward sometimes.
Time is both ward and warden. We are keys.

Rind

trace lines
around
my confusion

. . .

call it *skin*

Asterisks

What's the worst mistake you made in grad school?
I asked a room full of poets if any of them believed in ghosts.
—@elainecorden

I believe in ghosts.*

But around the time I started disclosing
my psychosis history to strangers and new friends
ten years after my diagnosis, I stopped saying so.
In my youth they shifted
at the corners of my eyelids, tucked
into moving shadows.
My teenage bedroom was in
my parents' basement, where
an intimidating entity haunted
from behind the cast iron woodstove.
I made a habit of saying hi
as I passed, to be polite.

*I don't get to claim psychosis *and* ghosts.
You can't have both.

The future predicted itself, and I haunted me.
Briefly I thought other ghosts haunted me, but it was just me.

The Grapefruit: Zip!

I press my hands through cotton, silk, polyester.
Fling a dress on the warm trample of sheets.
Step into my robe. Night falls away.

Being is a basic structure in time: a zipper extending
all the way back, metal teeth on an infinite throat.

The past a straight line reaching, arms spread
to a constellation of futures, closing on *one*.
Before us, fluid possibility. Past eats future.

The grapefruit is heavy as a breast in my hands, at the sink
faucet's stream. I am here, weighing the thin chain
of my life and washing my breakfast. My past may stud me
in my sleep, but now it's far away, and I have a bowl
and a spoon and I'm at the screen door, and the robin.

Mental Kaleidoscope: Where There's Wood There's Fire

mind cut coils

...

malformed idea
topiary fantasy
pre-verbal
emerald aura
heart-shaped vesicle
pop-rocks popsicle
magic ointment
split sapling
germinate
root-cutting
caterpillar tent ablaze
grim cloud formation
we are tempted but *no*
visual abomination
sweet whuff
latent fear
unwinding
itchy thought
double helix origins
empty shelves

a cut mind coils
like tongue around cavity

Domestic, Disordered

Into the coffee table's glossy surface
I scratch a vicious gasp.
I lay myself down to cry on the hard planes
of the house. Yesterday he broke tufts of indica
and left them there, like last week.
In this photo I have a broom in my hand.
In this one I don't.
In this photo I can't tell time.
Did he out me and discuss my daily failures?
I forget how to brush my hair.
I forget how to wash.
Unlearning his likes wasn't my intent, but
it was easier than tending the orchid,
whose blooms dropped.
I no longer see the *o*, the dimple, in his cheek.
The cat came back punctured and ticked.
Yesterday he left me here, last week.

The Grapefruit: Alarm

Gale-force winds tip the building,
shaking men from balconies like peas from
a colander. The ones who hurt me are wailing.

My alarm—it pulls.

I grab a T-shirt from the closet, slide open
a drawer, lift out my light-blue jeans, kitten-belly
denim fuzz. A ring in my ears. I put on my robe
and pass through screen door to back porch, barefoot.

Sun on skin.
Hum tune.
Go inside.

Today's echoes are loud. I can gut the child
of sweet orange and pomelo

but can't separate
then from *now*,
pith from flesh.

Desires accumulate like burrs.
Not once in my life have I stopped loving a person.
My disruptive sighs flower the apartment endlessly.

Swimmingly

Early in the summer of 2008—a very good year—I attempt suicide spontaneously in the kitchen.

I'm in third year in Toronto and sharing the four-bedroom apartment with my best friends V and JB.

Our walk-up apartment, known for its orange door on busy Dundas Street a few blocks east of the square, sits across streetcar tracks from a 24-hour Hasty Market. I buy two brunette wigs from the hair shop next to Hasty's, one shoulder-length and sleek, one longer and thicker, for when I don't feel like being a salon blonde.

I'm dating the first guy I *like*-like since high school, and when he introduces me at parties as his girlfriend, I tell him not to do that yet. I'm feeling good about myself.

Silent Lake and Pretty Palimpsests

> *But the dark pines of your mind dip deeper*
> *And you are sinking, sinking, sleeper*
> *In an elementary world;*
> *There is something down there and you want it told.*
> —Gwendolyn MacEwen, "Dark Pines Under Water"

When our minds go, they go to calm. The calm leaps into unknowns as though to be human were to be bread, sliced and bagged. What are we but eager to be swallowed? Who are we but sisters a-twitch along a metal-green surface like water striders? You are treading, skimming, scrolling, *but the dark pines of your mind dip deeper*

and the murk rises like a silt evening dress to suffocate you in a pool awash with the LEDs' glow, where the sound of water, its love songs for minnows, binds us all wriggling in a cone-shaped trap, *and you are sinking, sinking, sleeper*

in the mind's eye of men who would rub you out, toss you to the blurred below. Then, jagged up, stunned into submission like a sparkling muskie thumping the ribs of their boats, you hear them whisper through the cover of code and avatar. They say we're not that hard to catch. We're not that hard to fuck, marry, or kill. But try keeping us quiet—we talk chaos magic *in an elementary world;*

if we are echo only, what sonic boom will shock the gloom right out of this place? You hold your breath underwater. It's where you go when *there is something down there and you want it told.*

Characteristics of Nonlinear Systems

The past is an influenza fevering
photos
of the body.

The past is a flue congested,
coated by
the rising body.

The past is a mysterious cold spot
appearing
in the body.

A rhyme is how the past
ripples
through the body.

A memory is how

the ground gives,
soft underfoot

is how
feet disintegrate soft into
the ground

When Blossom Is an Ugly Word

My death started as a seed. As the piece of gum in my sixteen-year-old bush after the girl I loved tongue-weaved my first orgasm into me. As the light in the tiled bathroom of her parents' basement, the gum, pink and wet. As the bed where I returned to her. She asked why I was shaking. As the chemistry homework we'd finished earlier on the carpeted basement floor, or maybe it was the kitchen table, and our nerdy gusto for balancing chemical equations. As the notes we passed in class. As the next time, and the next time. As a secret. As a silent, hidden heartbreak. As the 2005 same-sex marriage debate and my family's Catholic priest telling parishioners to write letters to the federal government. As a midnight tide changing too late. As suicidal ideation I fashioned into survival alcoholism: morning vodka dribbled into chocolate milk cartons in the cache of my locker. As the belief I wouldn't make it past seventeen. The odd feeling when I did. As the words X told me that weekend back home in second year: how alike we were, *on s'entend bien*. As the makeshift bed on the floor. As pretending to fall asleep when he wanted more. As the incoming text, days later: *X killed himself*. As my body remembering his hands, his mouth, and thank god we didn't do it, as his body cloven by the train. As my conviction that young, old, or ancient,

I would be my own harvester too.

Hysteresis

Hysteresis is the name
for stress in an organism
or an object when effects
of the stressor

                                    lag.

Soil remembers the constriction of glaciers
and pushes up bitter white strawberries.

The band of my new Calvin Klein shelf bra
loosens and ripples until it barely
touches my ribc

                    age.

Brute

Hysteresis is the past

g
ripping the body.

Seriously, It's All Going Splendidly

I'm drinking, clubbing, having fun. I'm halfway through *The Brothers Karamazov*.

Double-decker buses rumble past my bedroom at eye level, the afternoons. Tourists' voices jump into me. A blurred blue

circle marks the wall across from my floor-length mirror, dyed by my ass dancing in jeans.

The kitchen leads to a spacious patio where I've planted flowers and long grasses in square wicker baskets. We keep our trash out there. We have a raccoon problem. The slanted rooftop is perfect for perching with a pack of Camel Blues and a Moleskine journal. My first attempt will earn me

a week in St. Michael's psych ward and the diagnosis of bipolar disorder 1 with psychotic features.

A figure, crouching, atop the wardrobe every summer haunts me.

When the transport truck went by with a passenger behind the cab, that was not an unknown ghost lost to the long road—

that was me haunting me.

Hallway Cynosure

Whenever I try to put words to the delusion that permanently changed my perception of time, I see the space at the top of the stairs of the Dundas Street apartment in between the kitchen and JB's bedroom door. Dusty corners: cat fur, clouds of fallen hair. Woodgrain? A railing. Weeks later I will break a friend-of-a-friend's nose as he braces himself on that railing, threatens violence and refuses to leave. The crack snaps like a glow stick. His blood whips out like silly string. It's the spot in the apartment with the least light, like the dark converges there. The day slants toward it from south, west, north, its sheen almost blue across the hardwood.

Cento for Pyrokinesis

What is real is taking the unreal,
what's to come—exhaust smog
like doubts upon the world, acting as if
the front door slamming and
undulating in the cool airstream
scraping the lavender sky
nestles round the scalp a vague thing, a pity object,
a wreath the colour of
howling light.

Jaclyn Desforges, "Freeze" / Chris Johnson, "If only we felt the same about *Mad Max: Fury Road* …" / Michael Mirolla, "The Listeners" / Stuart Ross, "Collected Poems" / Sonnet L'Abbé, "Going Back" / Paul Lisson, "Fourth Inevitability" / Claudia Coutu Radmore, "fluther of jellyfish" / Pearl Pirie, *Not Quite Dawn* / Grace Lau, "The Next Time You Scold My Body"

God Is a New Anchor Dipped into the Sea

I was surrounded by good things,
curtains of wake: do gods

abide barnacles
afraid of immensity

I couldn't get my bearings
until I touched bottom, self-sabotaged

newly sucking their iron
god-mother, suckling

shine in the slip of water?—a god
is a dipped thing,

but the bottom
rang my bones;

I saw shapes in my pain
tethered to cloud.

it need not be a straight course
I lifted   *when I was ready to feel weight,*

ho! to be faithful.
powerful hook:

is this aching, exuberant steel
the eye of the world?

Chatoyant

It's delusion only because I lift myself from our mutual system of reality. My mind sees what *now* means. I contain my past, present and future, existing simultaneously. I'm complete. I have access to all my timeline. Imagine a core sample drilled from the earth, marbled cylinder. Except it's flat like the moon. And like the moon, not edgeless. The space between rungs of my crib where I kick away from the wall. The storm sewer at the end of my childhood street, the slightly larger opening after the seventh bar; I squeeze through it to catch salamanders and crush leeches with rocks. The lovers one night or forever all the same to me. A piercing through of elations, a bed of nails. Successes yet to come. And there's the suicide on the far edge fated for me; I am myself, old, doing it. This flattening sets me plainly on the level of my destiny. So I do what heartbreak years before programmed me to do.

Cento for Clairvoyance

How is the hyacinth's bent head wrong?

If the pollen is heaved
        notoriously promiscuous
from the stupor of married sleep

or the merest shake
straps disclosure and violence together in ways
papaya can't distinguish

the future will be luminous and reckless
and in my mouth: the froth.

Roxanna Bennett, "Curse of the Hyacinth" / Doyali Islam, "33rd Parallel" / Christine McNair, "the problem of orchids" / Nancy Lee, "Alphas" / Frances Boyle, "handle with care" / Amber Dawn, "touch ≠ touch screen" / Caroline Szpak, "Allostatic Load" / Paul Lisson, "Awaiting the arrival of the butcher" / Elana Wolff, "Cord"

Transection

I text my friends: *I love you.* I go down to the Hasty Market for a regular-sized bottle of Advil and gulp the whole thing in the kitchen. My pink-pearl flip phone buzzes on the countertop. The guy I'm dating wants to come see me. *I can't explain why I just can't see you right now.* In the hospital bed under the spherical camera, he'll tell me he thought I was cheating when I sent that. The pills don't work, so I buy another. And another. And another. The shy clerk at first refuses to sell me the fourth, but I insist. My friend is *very* sick. I don't know why this satisfies him, but I've always been good at convincing people who could help me

I'm doing better than I am.

I cross the street eight times—the last two are extra strength—empty each vessel into me.

Mental Kaleidoscope: Where There's Fire There's Glass

twists mind to Sick Express

open concept
brute window
jewel mania addiction
flirtation
black turtleneck cult
intellectual darling
as seen in stripes
two columns
outline neatly structured
nerves on nerves
raw data transferring
be kind to us poets
though shiny, resilient
we will not be protected
by the giants we read
cockroach under a rocks glass
wound on display
threaded fisheye
open letdown
write sad
chlorinated sky

my sick mind twists to express
emotion: indignity a clasp to be loosed

Estuary

I have known myself
to worry
whether it is possible
for a mind / *freshwater*

to be so open
it falls right
out / *brine*

On Friendship

V comes downstairs to check on me—she'll later say she had a weird feeling—and finds me out cold on my face in front of the fridge. She wakes JB, who calls the ambulance. When they guide me to the orange door, I want to wear my dancing heels. They don't let me. I don't remember this. JB will tell me I flipped her off from the stretcher in the back of the emergency truck.

Manic Wire

Do you like my braids? Pinterest taught me.
Curls come tumbling.
I have a room just for this. Night terrors and vanity.
Pigeons, *rroux rroux.*
Rroux, rroux. It sounds like American poets.
Sounds like opaque familiarity.

Words can be barriers to define self, concisely.

Call me modal (a helping verb): domestic, gullible.
Or fierce. Woo me. Count me among the wombed
wombing. Periodically cocooning.

Time flattens.

Medication insulates the raw copper wire.

Do something about heavy doorways.
Push or something.

Curtains could be plusher, tender.
Fear the slender monster where the waves
part ways.
Light.

Keep out light
-hearted nurses with their blue
triage forms.

Scratchy upholstering.
Too many beeps to calm down.
What is it to have this body?

High, a ceiling light,
or a spent weapon, holstered.

Little Woman

My pale scalp turns black. My cuticles and under my nails too. Gums and teeth and lips and nose: black. A manuscript pulled from a fire. The girl who tries suicide comes back sooty as hell. It's charcoal, used to pump my stomach. I remember the bathroom where I first see myself and try to scrub it off—standard hospital bathroom, round corners, calming lights. To orient myself in the maze-like hospital, I remember which side of the wall I face the mirror in. Left. *That way.*

Wherever I go. There I—

Cloudtops whipped stiff like eggs and sugar, white on blue.
Imagine: splintering bones, crushed earth and fuselage, ribs
piercing red gore, liver, colon, kidney.

My desire to live haunted me. I refused to write this line
until we landed. I was crossing this large body of water

to lift a curse.

Lith Poem

1. SUN-DIM, P.M.

plump pill   tummy plinth
                              acne nation

lithium carbonate latte, 900 mg, take

three capsules daily

now put the foundation under them
                              take with food
                    may cause drowsiness or bad business

2. MON-LUN, A.M.

let thee, um, pills fill throat   pelican
salt beats illness, water beats salt
a needle goes into me   test blood toxicity
          trimonthly
how do you hone disorder?
coke fizz saturated yet?
          test
narrow therapeutic index, sample drawn
from a vein   med levels
somewhere between permasleep and dilated mind

3. TUE-MAR, A.M.

send quote to irritated stomach
email receipt to   anxiety portal
take with food

prep   Zoom spoons
send edit to do not stop tx w/o medical supervision
send Qs to   doom-doom   I hope this can be a growth
                                awareness moment

4. WED-MER, P.M.

"there is a natural product that could
help with error terror darkness   calumny
              defamation   and slander"

super, thanks

5. THURS-JEU, A.M.

what do you call a jiggly gold slimy

    moon stuck under each tired eye?

self éclair

6. FRI-VEN, P.M.

kissy hum pill   cinch Saturn
thrill stabilizer   mayor of shhh   sway   go away

"are you ever gonna reply?"

ideal wife   ideal wife   vaxed n waxed

let's yum

violently angry at the baseball diamond

fragrant enough

icky

if I miss a dose of lithium

icky if I dehydrate
take too much

7. SAT-SAM, P.M.

"we" again

ever good at making up
even did some flips
to be more welcoming

8. SUN-DIM, A.M.

frogs also do takeout
too much sometimes

sample thimble sensations
limp   simple thump
heart to pull out
from that which is about (to) take form (hypo, mania)
magnets like me suffer from cravings to possess
& magnify

puppy pill   make wag-happy
this completely disengaged & dispassionate
rainbow
flat

is flatness just the confidence that we'll survive
anything, or die?

Dear Rue

From the first episode of *Euphoria* you tell it straight:
bipolar's a baseline discomfort.
Correction by meds taught you
to seek spectral highs, the gateway
not weed but prescription. Chemistry
tidy as glitter bombs. You got out of rehab
on summer break and going back
to friends they said *I thought your ass*
was dead. Huh. To rise dancing from a pool of vomit
only to be shunned. How even Mischa Barton
said of Marissa Cooper: *My character*
has been through so, so much and there's really

nothing more left
for her to do.

I'm pretty sure you'd stand with me
and say, Mischa, screw you. Rue, I want to say
I've never felt so seen on a TV screen.
And I love the way you love your sister fierce.
I swigged your glee when you fired rounds into a bound
and blazing villain. I smelled the gasoline.
What plane are you on? Of existence?
I know you're fiction but I'm grateful you exist.

Was staying blonde good luck or bad luck?
Was my bad luck always good luck?

As I write this poem, I revisit me.

Learning Curve

> *I designed my own passivity, I present it to you by my face, by your guts, and in the name of human space. I was born into a rough little city, site of hasty invention actively dissolving into steel sky. The city was a glittering ruin sucked upwards.*
>
> —Lisa Robertson, "Early Education"

Because my mind went, I went to books. Because I went to books my mind didn't go *too* far. These receptacles pour into and out of each other. Two tongues, kissing. I kept it for me at first, this hexagonal knowledge, expensive rutting of grammar between my ears. Years ago, *I designed my own passivity, I present it to you by my face, by your*

sweater, mucked and trodden, your cough and esophagus, his cells under your fingernails. A culvert swells with salamanders, storm sewage over thighs. Soft metal pine needles, bed of thieves. What bad spirits in milky swamps do: splay *guts, and in the name of human space. I was born into a rough*

system of dominance. Perpetual scroll of bodies: buckwheat-zucchini bikini bodies, tennis-tan bodies, hairy-pubis bodies, smooth-boned bodies, glazed chunky donuts, telling me I am beautiful, showing me I am ugly, intelligent app itching to turn my skin into a lens, all-seeing body void of pores and valleys. Yesterday, I learned your name, floated on a screen. Bottle flies rooting in the mud of your *little city, site of hasty invention actively dissolving into steel sky.*

Because you couldn't speak I went to speak. What we did with trees here. We bent and echoed, bent and flailed arms. A lamppost flickered our souls made of eels, we travelled on land and through water. A car turned its beams on the procession. We were speaking in text at last: intruded writing bodies, penetrated bodies, powerful names hanging from points of entry bodies, ginger ale bodies fizzing with anger, stifled-career bodies, chokecherry bodies, bodies choosing to be naked if shame is all there is to wear, and the parade laughed and cried, and *the city was a glittering ruin sucked upwards.*

Schoolyard Trick

We were inducted into the pen club

then walked around with *penis* in blue
on forearm, an introductory curse;

a warning about boys mistaking our
propensity for penmanship

with a passion for all wands.

Mechanisms

Note the trajectory of words
upon whose curvature anger rises and recedes

in correlation to the distance
between those projectiles and his body.

I have a history: strong reactions to gendered slights.
I attack when I know *he* won't kill me.

Why hurt, why touch at all
if not with compassion?

It may be years since the last trauma
but sanctuary comes slow as hair.

This love is mittens: soft, needed, unravelling.

The Tulips' Eyes Are Xs

When the dream gets violent,

you step up to villainy
and all your rapists are dead now.

Meaty disconnected heads
lopped like tulips in the yard.

You are terrified of the person
you've become.

You are not a merciful hole.

You cannot say in the poem
the things you've done
while sleeping.

It's okay to be afraid.

Gasping at the blue splotch of paint on the ceiling above the marriage bed, I haunted me solo with pleasure, creating the future through that blue error.

I closed my eyes, midafternoon, pictured myself elsewhere.

Circuits

Perception, in whatever sensory modality, is the result of the brain's cartographic skill. The brain maps the world and it maps the body. These maps, and the relationships between them, form the perceptual content of our lives. The mapped body is in intercourse, from birth to death, with the mapping brain, and even as the world impresses itself upon us, these maps permanently change the bodies from which they arise. Consciousness is a feedback loop. The self-creating self is an atlas.

Assessment Questionnaire

after Sina Queyras's "Numb is more natural"

Who is livid, who is more *spear* than *remember*? Who is behind the cumulonimbus? Who remembers being behind? Who feels torrential, recalling the cumulonimbus? Who is willing to listen? Who tumbles? Who is exactly how tender they wanted to be? Who is a pall of sleep? Who's been having discussions on the radio? Who is not yet a mother and scattered? Who is too much a bother and afraid? Who sees themselves a tremor? Who sways? Who devastates? Whose feet throb? Whose tummy hurts? Whose nose itches? Who has a shelfful of poets? Who hastens to despots? Who sees violet peripheral flashes? Who looks like lemons, sucking? Whose cochleae triage praise? Who misses kissing? Who, brimless? Who, barricaded? Who has yet to break even? Who has broken acrylics? Who wakes to tremors? Who makes vases of their face? Who swears puddles turn into cats? Who swallows oysters whole? Who chews? Who's felt bird bones? Who mingles with long-dead dictators? Who is adjusting? Who is loud enough?

Whose limbo is dancing in front of them?

Erasure

When I learned I "killed" him
well, I gave the sky my mouth
                    and laughed

                    Only ever met him once,
                    My friend's older brother's friend
                    I was nearly seventeen

On the bus to school Monday, I—
there's, what? it's only flashes

His room   his
                        -ide me Disoriented
                    panicking, pricked, loud with fear

a strip of vertical light at the door
                    He shushed me. "   ,"

His jeans
crumpled next to mine

He
drove
me
home

Calm down: his repetition
in the room,
in the dark.

When for months I scratched sores in my scalp and raised scabs, that wasn't me haunting me.

Wreck

I found his obituary online

tragic
car
accident

man, 24, plowed into and under

                    a tractor trailer
                    his roof and windshield sheared

Other girls. (He did the same to them)
But I'd wanted to move on

                    He died
                    Psychosis, my own
                    mineral power

Innate and magical
Vengeance   sting of yellow sulphur, burnt powder
Sentient smoke
                    undulates like bath tresses

or tinfoil
or steel

I could have reported him but never did
I could have
changed / let
his / him
life / live

When I learned I "killed" him
well, I laughed

Overlay

I superpose where I am now to that old brain map of the hospital. On my right, my husband, sleeping. To my left, my reading lamp casts a glow over the chair where I keep my belongings handy for nighttime. The white paint's worn down to the chair's wood. Twin blue bees with long abdomens are stamped on the top rail with the words BEES & QUEENS. On the seat, my phone, pill organizer, bottle of zopiclone, Vaseline for dry feet, to-do list notebook, monthly planner, highlighter, pen, floral clipboard, mason jar of water, bullet vibrator, AirPods case, and Jessi MacEachern's *A Number of Stunning Attacks*. The corner of window, a flutter of beige zebra-print curtain. That's where that hospital mirror would be if rooms in my memory existed here: above the chair, behind the light, next to the window. Quick left turn to my almost-death.

Psychosis is a living metaphor.
Late at night, the walls emanate radio music.
Patterns erupt like nerves.

Tactile Hallucination

A balloon the shape of my body expanded in me, filling rounded corners with my square insides. I didn't like the pressure.

Harm Done

A nurse with contempt
in his veins.

Did he have a clipboard?
Did he check my pulse?

I was alone with him
in a small, dim room. He told me
if I'd really wanted to kill myself,
I would've used
██████ instead.

The Forest

is never like glass
except in winter,
when it is inside us
crackling with a roughness
only trees know.

Even seamless silicone
requires permission
into breakable flesh.

There is one more monster
with a nose and two eyes,
making women into trees.

If there is justice
let us be impenetrable
or let us shatter—not this
resilient, speechless wound.

Again One Year Later, an Evening in June

1.

I bike to the Hasty Market in front of my old apartment.
Buy four pill bottles and a jug of juice.
Sit on the sidewalk beside the door, lit up.
First the sleeping pills, lithium, half an oxy.
Then, I cram the white pills down.

Vomit splatters gravel. Flecked, thick and shining.
I didn't mean to puke them up.
I scoop the bile and pills off the sidewalk
and eat them again.

The clerk, the same one as the summer before, runs to me
so tall, his head cocked out the door, and calls 911.

{i}

The moon, ajar, swallows pills
in the vertical light outside
the convenience store

and   heaves all over the sidewalk

clouds solid as hands collect the orange
liquid   pills (stars
                                clustered)
dirt and crystal-pinging acid, sour grit

Mercury, too fast, in a collared shirt
grabs a telephone corded to the cash
Come to us, truck of mercy, we are at risk

But the moon seeks eclipse, not salvation

2.

The lengths I go not to fail this time.
This horror story: cupping the street to my face.
There was a weedy space between the orange-door
apartment and the next-door restaurant. Overgrown.
A fence had been put up. When I first sat streetside
I thought to climb there so no one could find me.
But the pills were too quick, and so was the clerk.

{ii}

The moon's mouth is a lake expanding
into recesses, other sides
never lit, a thousand potato eyes
a mouth and hands converging
where the sick

exits then enters, cumulonimbus passes
over her   face, alarmthickness drips
She must not waste the medicine

There is a carpet of grass
between two buildings
whose shadow the moon never reaches

The moon couldn't dip low enough to hide
like an injured animal bows its head
to greet death,   alone

3.

Seeing stars. Pulsing above me.
Like Christmas string lights reflected
in puddles post-holiday.
Pretty twinkling orbs. I was out
before they strapped me in
and sirened me away.

{iii}

The ambulance arrives, the moon
blinks away stars who are plankton, poison
treasured, round, lifted from the flat surface

of cement in the up-down
violet light, flashes
sunspots, flares   scoops
all that orange sickness
up, gulped, gaseous giants onlooking

The moon: sped away, stars wink
at EMTs across the box.
Entropy a siren wagging her split tail.

With each new fracture, I haunted myself anew. I stood at the mirror, studying the image, couldn't see my neon thoughts. Over and over, I didn't die, and not dying *haunted me.*

Cento for Immortality

i.

The first time was in the middle of a thunderstorm.
In the parking lot you declared:

Medicine begins with losing a name,
completely inadequate language of sorrow.

If I know what forever means,
what is it that I fear exactly? The emptiness, or

the light coming through painted flowers.
I am tired. Everyone's tired of my turmoil.

I don't want to be an old woman. But why not? I was sexy.
    I don't want to die.
A doorway only reminds me what I can't cross.

ii.

Wonder when the non-sense will slow,
tossing word salad on the tongue

like silver bags of crispy chips.
I embraced the fantastic,

and embarrassment, your thumb back and forth
in my sadness

and I could tell you
phrases I know so well that my subconscious has spoken it

raw. Meet norm, custom, habit, manner, rule, order, law.
I do not want to know them.

iii.

Till medication can herd thoughts
and the awkwardness of their

fear hovering between two ways—
they're fine monsters

to be isolated & recorded
like a length of rope, fixing

to tinker with our failed time machines, physics of regret
never reaching terminus.

They slide over me and fit like thigh-highs;
each drug that numbs alerts another nerve to pain.

iv.

Deaths   a suicide   or several   (women)
if stopped, we dared to risk, grab the ligaments of chance

and speak our collective prophecy
and set us tingling through a thousand threads.

What does it mean to actively die? Actively?
"Death has a life of its own," he says.

Didn't their fate speak quietly to you?
How are you still here breathing working hustling like a motherfucker

You conceal your shame like sunset pollen
in the itch of quotation marks.

v.

Does it always feel
like rungs, memorizing their faces,

picking the soft scab of radiation above the bruise?
Do you hear the thunder of

the ordinariness of the waves, the scar debating
in silence the silence ajar

How many memories can one fit into the palm of now?
Kumquat. Snail. Fuzzy peach.

Consciousness cannot be rated.
I offer to sing for you instead.

i: MA|DE, "Vertical Logic at the Crossroads of the World" / Nancy Lee, "Dogs" / Elee Kraljii Gardiner, "Tunica Intima" / Frances Boyle, "Sort of an Elegy: iii. Wake" / Terese Mason Pierre, "A New Face" / Sina Queyras, "Years" / Kim Fahner, "Paintings for Sale" / Robert Lowell, "Eye and Tooth" / Brenda Shaughnessy, "Notes on an Old Holiday" / Manahil Bandukwala, "Threshold Ghazal" ii: Claudia Coutu Radmore, "in a giraffe's armpit" / Klara du Plessis and Khashayar "Kess" Mohammadi, "Vestigium" / Anna Van Valkenburg, "Little Red in Love" / Helen Robertson, *body of stone* / Molly Cross-Blanchard, "Granville Island" / Anna Van Valkenburg, "The Truth Is" / Ashley Hynd, "as seen by the distance" / Amber Dawn, "fountainhead" / Susan Gillis, "Obelisk" / Sandra Ridley, "Thicket"

iii: Khashayar "Kess" Mohammadi, "God Gone Astray in the Flesh" / Christine McNair, "in matia" / Jim Johnstone, "The King of Terrors" / Hollay Ghadery, "Chair Pose" / Jessi MacEachern, "Notes on Moving" / Nancy Lee, "Husbandry" / Nancy Lee, "For the Next Person Who Asks (How We Balance Teaching and Writing)" / D.S. Stymeist, "Mass Transfer Pass. 6 & 7" / Ellen Chang-Richardson, "P. T." / Robert Lowell, "Soft Wood"

iv: Hoa Nguyen, "Vietnam Ghost Story: Towers of District 5" / Oana Avasilichioaei, "If" / Helen Robertson, "Sybilant S" / Robert Lowell, "The Flaw" / Liz Howard, "Letter from Halifax" / Rebecca Păpucaru, "Prevention" / Rainer Maria Rilke, trans. by Edward Snow, "The First Elegy" / Barbara Jane Reyes, "Brown Girl Fields Many Questions" / Kama La Mackerel, "existence as gender survivance" / Caroline Szpak, "Astrobleme Anodyne"

v: Conyer Clayton, "Distracted Backs" / Shira Erlichman, "The Runner" / Michael Mirolla, "Blind Alley" / natalie hanna, "house" / Canisia Lubrin, "Act VII: Ain't I Again?" / Cameron Anstee, "St. Andrew Voices" / Sachiko Murakami, "Still, Here" / Kirby, "What Do You Want to Be Called?" / Angela Hibbs, "There Are a Thousand Ways to Get Over Yourself" / Stuart Ross, "A Pretty Good Year"

Surf Lessons

It was a sprouted need, this plant with teeth,
true Venus. Fuck the rage that boils us, bleeds us.

This is a healing spell: bream green,
and foam dries in lipped petals

delicate as the conversations
with the ones we've hurt.

On Tylenol and Other Pills

The day after my second attempt, thirst breaks me. I beg but am not allowed water. A nurse unwraps a sucky lemon stick, warns water could kill me. This need is animal, hairy. Alone behind a curtain, from my hospital bed, catheter-tethered, I grab a pulp kidney dish, stretch to fill it from the sink, and guzzle.

A doctor informs me acetaminophen death is excruciating, that organ shutdown takes days to kick in. Three days until pain, of *can't take it back*. Pills the domain of the impulsive: least likely to grim but most likely to havoc. A bad way to go, or not go.

In night's deep, a welcome voice visits. A volunteer chaplain. I tell the stranger my secret joys from this secret side, still dying

yet wishing to live.

I am old and aimless as the sun, and just as radiant.

Regeneration

I am my chipping manicure. Moons peek
from under gel, expensive
crescents push out dead keratin,
rejecting last week's body.

I am my chapped lips: skin

that once grew skin that once touched skin
that once held breath and blood and knees once skinned.

I am my skim breath.

I am everything
off the top
and what's underneath.

I am not my haircut.
I am not splitting hairs.

I am not my boots, not the sum of blocks
walked on the way to and from my workplace,
not my workplace. I am not my work.

I am cell renewal, membranes kissing
within my body project:

tongue and speech turn
silence inside out—look, grace.

There was a resoluteness to my decisions, particularly where sex was involved. When an intervention became necessary, I haunted me. Some small objects were strategically moved, a set of keys, for one. The danger felt immense yet negligible. Washing dishes helped.

Subdued

after rob mclennan's "Subtitled, [a primer]"

Below cranium, indelible murmurs. Create
islands between pulses. Medicated
fallow. Dunes. Elsewhere,

trace the dunes.

Lack, or thoughtless. No vivid dreams.

Withdraw. A bed is made of switching limbs.
Slip a tab onto tongue before sleep.

A meal the shape
of sheep.

But, the fires. Fire.

What distant sparks
have been glinting?

Like an Old Closet Door, the Inevitable Pops Out of Its Groove

I exit Toronto Western Hospital polka-dotted with ECG glue. Newsstands line the street, front-page celebrity deaths. What golden filament is this? My fate, dislodged. My parents take me to their hotel. Now, swim the indoor pool, cosmic. Body of skin, tiny bikini, mini bubbles suck pores, grey circles sticky in chlorinated water.

Air Show

the sky's hot   metal

wing presses   into uterus

a compression   in the grass

                    where the world should be

          an open palm shudders under

the blue   outstretched

for tender   or a kiss

My Speech Has Nice Flowers

but some days when I am tired
I forget the good words for flowers
and all I have are curl, piston
stamen, yellow

I mean pistil

phlox

there's one
and honeysuckle

stripe

Good days and bad
silk hydrangeas
gather dust

they always
look so
fresh

If Post-Attempt Psychiatric Care Were Sweet

It couldn't be
biscotti, *baked twice.*
The dough rolled out,
blanched almonds
and chocolate chips,
baked not browned,
on the counter
sliced, then back
in the oven again.
The attention required.

It's not comforting
like chocolate mayonnaise cake,
that subtle tang
celebration's flavour.
We'd eat it warm
from the oven, spoon
butter icing over to melt.
How cake translates
to *you are loved.*

It wouldn't be
grocery-store lemon
meringue pie.
Simple, cheap,
available.

It turns out
when it comes to
surviving suicide
there's no dessert at all
except surviving suicide.

Mermaid and Fisherman Seven Years into Marriage

Pry open the clams. Ask them if I was free.

I didn't realize how bad you were.

I was in love. And I told you what I was.

You needed to find your footing.

Your cracked hands were like moonlight prying.

I thought you were a jellyfish.

My allure, incandescent?

Yeah, likely to sting.

Love is foam, each of us a bubble.

Have you ever been to a foam party? I was a shooter girl in a bikini and heels selling Jell-O shots I squirted into mouths with a giant plastic syringe.

Who was I back then, at nineteen?
Is she still in here, haunting me?

Blackberries

A grasshopper thuds in flight: my scapula.
My shoulder aches thanks to pavement's pull.
My tibia: a mongoose hiding in all this flesh,
hoarding eggs. My throat: a highway, surging.
So why can't I speak? The warm bath
of time   floats around me, cooling.
I am always leaving: the being beyond the word.
My kneecaps are heartbeats, hibernating bears.
Phalanges: fish spines laid out along a sandy lake.
Blood clots run through me monthly
like so many blackberries. Firefly children
test the word *mother* before I   wake.
Smother fire before it burns the curtains. An abyss
beyond that word's promise: mother. *Parent*?
What about platelet? Or blood not mixed, or bones
not formed? What shaky instrument do I have
with which to prolong life? Hips? That's it?

Hysterosonogram

I have seen three perinatal psychiatrists
this month; each one's advice
goes against the others'
and everything I've been warned about
for a decade.

Their questions of my history make me
red with light inside. It aches.
I wear a sheet while the doctor
inserts a catheter, balloon.

On the monitor my uterus: a planet
where hurt is the mother tongue.
Light skidding over valleys and ridges: a site
resistant to damage.

Light blipping over ova and striated flesh:
pomegranate gems.

Afterward, a neighbourhood walk.
The five p.m. sun will slick
eavestroughs golden, starburst windows.
I will bring my face into the flares
above the hard snow,

my body booming
with old griefs.

I was told there would be pain.
It's not the pain I remember.
The pain I remember hooks like light
through an open stitch.

Ahead, in the sky, a percussion of pigeons.
Ahead, in the street, a leashed dog.

Window View from Childhood Bedroom after Betrayal

Cloud-ragged night, bisected by stars.
Habits reset through the eye of a dream.

Thought's edge, like a claw,
rankles morning's paisley blanket
of the home to which I've retreated.

A spare, sturdy varnished desk by the bed.

Down the hall, my great-aunt's budgie
emits precise chirps, lasers of sound.
I learned this week only the males speak.

Only the boys have a spot of blue above their beaks.
Aunt Ursula and I discuss her favourite TV show,
90 Day Fiancé. She suspects the pet shop swindler
took marker to her birdie's face.

Let's paint these feelings into small frames,
so we can move away with them, easily.

Entity

My parents' basement is a memory trove. Stuffed animals fill the wooden cradle my grandfather carved, where I slept as an infant. As I nose this dusty brain map, remembering the woodstove's cool surface, its creaking coil handle, the bat drowned in airless ash inside, I realize I am here

behind the stove's cast iron hulk. I am the haunting entity.

I am watching that teenage girl

tip her head to me, politely,

and say hi.

Self-love, turtledoves, mother's love,

all love is the terror kind.

My flowery sighs haunt the apartment, deathlessly.
Only, this time, there's a little fish inside me.

We'll swim the day in neurochemicals, venturing
beyond the screen door, into the glory-of-the-snow.

NOTES

Cento for Psychometry borrows lines from three source poems. In all of the centos in this collection, the words, word order, and italicizations of each line are identical to those in the source poem. Capitalization and punctuation may have been altered. In the lists below, the first numeral refers to the stanza; the second numeral refers to the line within the stanza.

1.1 Anna Van Valkenburg, "A Frozen Plum Tells Time," *Queen and Carcass* (Anvil Press, 2020).
1.2 Roxanna Bennett, "Waiting List," *Unmeaningable* (Gordon Hill Press, 2019).
1.3 Shira Erlichman, "Ghazal, Interrupted," *Odes to Lithium* (Alice James Books, 2019).

Cento for Pyrokinesis borrows lines from nine source poems.

1.1 Jaclyn Desforges, "Freeze," *Danger Flower* (Palimpsest Press, 2021).
1.2 Chris Johnson, "If only we felt the same about *Mad Max: Fury Road*..." *Listen, Partisan! And Other Stumbling Haibun* (Frog Hollow Press, 2016).
1.3 Michael Mirolla, "The Listeners," *Light and Time* (Guernica Editions, 2010).

1.4 Stuart Ross, "Collected Poems," *A Sparrow Came Down Resplendent* (Buckrider Books, 2016).
1.5 Sonnet L'Abbé, "Going Back," *A Strange Relief* (McClelland & Stewart, 2001).
1.6 Paul Lisson, "Fourth Inevitability," *The Perfect Archive* (Guernica Editions, 2019).
1.7 Claudia Coutu Radmore, "fluther of jellyfish," *camera obscura* (above/ground press, 2019).
1.8 Pearl Pirie, *Not Quite Dawn* (Éditions des petits nuages, 2020).
1.9 Grace Lau, "The Next Time You Scold My Body," *The Language We Were Never Taught to Speak* (Guernica Editions, 2021).

Cento for Clairvoyance borrows lines from nine source poems.

1.1 Roxanna Bennett, "Curse of the Hyacinth," *Unmeaningable* (Gordon Hill Press, 2019).
2.1 Doyali Islam, "33rd Parallel," *heft* (McClelland & Stewart, 2019).
2.2 Christine McNair, "the problem of orchids," *Charm* (Book*hug, 2017).
2.3 Nancy Lee, "Alphas," *What Hurts Going Down* (McClelland & Stewart, 2020).
3.1 Frances Boyle, "handle with care," *This White Nest* (Quattro Books, 2019).
3.2 Amber Dawn, "touch ≠ touch screen," *My Art Is Killing Me* (Arsenal Pulp Press, 2020).

3.3 Caroline Szpak, "Allostatic Load," *Slinky Naïve* (Anvil Press, 2018).
4.1 Paul Lisson, "Awaiting the arrival of the butcher," *The Perfect Archive* (Guernica Editions, 2019).
4.2 Elana Wolff, "Cord," *Everything Reminds You of Something Else* (Guernica Editions, 2017).

Lith Poem was written in study of Hoa Nguyen's sonically daring *A Thousand Times You Lose Your Treasure.*

Circuits borrows the following line from neuroscientist Antonio Damasio's *Self Comes to Mind: Constructing the Conscious Brain* (2010). "Perception, in whatever sensory modality, is the result of the brain's cartographic skill."

Cento for Immortality borrows lines from fifty source poems.

i.

1.1 MA|DE, "Vertical Logic at the Crossroads of the World," *A Trip to the ZZoo* (Collusion Books, 2020).
1.2 Nancy Lee, "Dogs," *What Hurts Going Down* (McClelland & Stewart, 2020).
2.1 Elee Kraljii Gardiner, "Tunica Intima," *Trauma Head* (Anvil Press, 2018).
2.2 Frances Boyle, "Sort of an Elegy: iii. Wake," *Light-carved Passages* (BuschekBooks, 2014).

3.1 Terese Mason Pierre, "A New Face," *Manifest* (Gap Riot Press, 2020).

3.2 Sina Queyras, "Years," *My Ariel* (Coach House Books, 2017).

4.1 Kim Fahner, "Paintings for Sale," *Emptying the Ocean* (Frontenac House, 2022).

4.2 Robert Lowell, "Eye and Tooth," *For the Union Dead* (Farrar, Straus and Giroux, 1964).

5.1 Brenda Shaughnessy, "Notes on an Old Holiday," *The Octopus Museum* (Alfred A. Knopf, 2019).

5.2 Manahil Bandukwala, "Threshold Ghazal," *Heliotropia* (Brick Books, 2024).

ii.

6.1 Claudia Coutu Radmore, "in a giraffe's armpit," *camera obscura* (above/ground press, 2019).

6.2 Klara du Plessis and Khashayar "Kess" Mohammadi, "Vestigium," *G* (Palimpsest Press, 2023).

7.1 Anna Van Valkenburg, "Little Red in Love," *Queen and Carcass* (Anvil Press, 2020).

7.2 Helen Robertson, *body of stone* (The Blasted Tree, 2021).

8.1 Molly Cross-Blanchard, "Granville Island," *Exhibitionist* (Coach House Books, 2021).

8.2 Anna Van Valkenburg, "The Truth Is," *Queen and Carcass* (Anvil Press, 2020).

9.1 Ashley Hynd, "as seen by the distance," *Entropy* (Gap Riot Press, 2020).

9.2 Amber Dawn, "fountainhead," *My Art Is Killing Me* (Arsenal Pulp Press, 2020).
10.1 Susan Gillis, "Obelisk," *Yellow Crane* (Brick Books, 2018).
10.2 Sandra Ridley, "Thicket," *Vixen* (Book*hug, 2023).

iii.

11.1 Khashayar "Kess" Mohammadi, "God Gone Astray in the Flesh," *Me, You, Then Snow* (Gordon Hill Press, 2021).
11.2 Christine McNair, "in matia," *Charm* (Book*hug, 2017).
12.1 Jim Johnstone, "The King of Terrors," *The King of Terrors* (Coach House Books, 2023).
12.2 Hollay Ghadery, "Chair Pose," *Rebellion Box* (Radiant Press, 2023).
13.1 Jessi MacEachern, "Notes on Moving," *A Number of Stunning Attacks* (Invisible Publishing, 2021).
13.2 Nancy Lee, "Husbandry," *What Hurts Going Down* (McClelland & Stewart, 2020).
14.1 Nancy Lee, "For the Next Person Who Asks (How We Balance Teaching and Writing)," *What Hurts Going Down* (McClelland & Stewart, 2020).
14.2 D.S. Stymeist, "Mass Transfer Pass. 6 & 7," *Cluster Flux* (Frontenac House, 2023).
15.1 Ellen Chang-Richardson, "P.T." *Unlucky Fours* (Anstruther Press, 2020).
15.2 Robert Lowell, "Soft Wood," *For the Union Dead* (1964).

iv.

16.1 Hoa Nguyen, "Vietnam Ghost Story: Towers of District 5," *A Thousand Times You Lose Your Treasure* (Wave Books, 2021).
16.2 Oana Avasilichioaei, "If," *Eight Track* (Talonbooks, 2019).
17.1 Helen Robertson, "Sybilant S," *body of stone* (The Blasted Tree, 2021).
17.2 Robert Lowell, "The Flaw," *For the Union Dead* (1964).
18.1 Liz Howard, "Letter from Halifax," *Letters in a Bruised Cosmos* (McClelland & Stewart, 2021).
18.2 Rebecca Păpucaru, "Prevention," *The Panic Room* (Nightwood Editions, 2017).
19.1 Rainer Maria Rilke, trans. by Edward Snow, "The First Elegy," *Duino Elegies* (North Point Press, 2000).
19.2 Barbara Jane Reyes, "Brown Girl Fields Many Questions," *Letters to a Young Brown Girl* (BOA Editions, 2020).
20.1 Kama La Mackerel, "existence as gender survivance," *ZOM-FAM* (Metonymy Press, 2020).
20.2 Caroline Szpak, "Astrobleme Anodyne," *Slinky Naïve* (Anvil Press, 2018).

v.

21.1 Conyer Clayton, "Distracted Backs," *We Shed Our Skin Like Dynamite* (Guernica Editions, 2020).

21.2 Shira Erlichman, "The Runner," *Odes to Lithium* (Alice James Books, 2019).
22.1 Michael Mirolla, "Blind Alley," *Light and Time* (Guernica Editions, 2010).
22.2 natalie hanna, "house," *infinite redress* (baseline press, 2020).
23.1 Canisia Lubrin, "Act VII: Ain't I Again?" *The Dyzgraphxst* (McClelland & Stewart, 2020).
23.2 Cameron Anstee, "St. Andrew Voices," *Sheets: Typewriter Works* (Invisible Publishing, 2022).
24.1 Sachiko Murakami, "Still, Here," *Render* (Arsenal Pulp Press, 2020).
24.2 Kirby, "What Do You Want to Be Called?" *What Do You Want to Be Called?* (Anstruther Press, 2020).
25.1 Angela Hibbs, "There Are a Thousand Ways to Get Over Yourself," *Control Suppress Delete* (Palimpsest Press, 2017).
25.2 Stuart Ross, "A Pretty Good Year," *A Sparrow Came Down Resplendent* (Buckrider Books, 2016).

ACKNOWLEDGEMENTS

Thank you to the publications in whose pages many of these poems have appeared in earlier forms: *Arc Poetry*, *Contemporary Verse 2*, *Dusie Tuesday*, disability lit anthology *The Ending Hasn't Happened Yet* (Sable Books, 2022), *The Ex-Puritan*, *Feminist Caucus in Conversation* chapbook (League of Canadian Poets, 2022), *GUEST*, *Non.Plus Lit*, *Paris Lit Up*, *Parenthesis Journal*, *periodicities*, LCP's Poetry Pause, *Rat's Ass Review*, *Room*, *talking about strawberries all of the time*, *The Temz Review*, *Touch the Donkey*, and *Train Journal*.

Thank you to Kama La Mackerel for selecting "Silent Lake and Pretty Palimpsests" as the winner of *Room*'s 2021 poetry contest and to *Room* for the prize, and thank you to Chelene Knight for shortlisting an earlier version of the suite about my suicide attempts for the *Fiddlehead*'s 2021 nonfiction contest.

Thank you to Guernica Editions and especially my editor and publisher Michael Mirolla, for giving *Ajar* a home and for your unflagging support of my literary work over the years.

Thank you Nithya Swaminathan for the use of your oil painting "Grapefruit Reflections on Pink" for *Ajar*'s cover, and to Rafael Chimicatti for the design.

Thank you to the freelance and chapbook editors who helped shape this manuscript along the way. Darby Minott Bradford for flow and authenticity of voice, Amber Dawn for clarity and care, Andy Verboom for economy and sound,

Shane Neilson for sculpting and curation resulting in my chapbook *In Violet*—and thank you Jim Johnstone and Erica Smith at Anstruther Press for publishing *In Violet*.

Thank you to my dear friends and early readers Conyer Clayton, Hollay Ghadery, Shira Nayman.

Thank you to Hollay for helping *Ajar* (and me) reach more eyes and ears with River Street Writing.

Thank you to my passionate and generous poetry and nonfiction professors Jen Ferguson, Susan Musgrave, Bronwen Tate, and all my UBC MFA peers who provided thoughtful feedback on earlier versions of these pieces in workshop.

Thank you to my VII crew with whom life is astoundingly fuller, more meaningful, more fun. You are my best friends, my inspiration, my community and collaborators, the group chat, my lifeline: Manahil Bandukwala, Ellen Chang-Richardson, Conyer Clayton, nina jane drystek, Chris Johnson, Helen Robertson.

Thank you to my lively Ottawa poetry community.

Thank you to the cento'd and glossed poets whose lines of poetry I've repurposed and whose books opened inner doors for me.

Thank you to the Ontario Arts Council for the Literary Creation grant and the Recommender Grants for Writers, and to Brick Books, *Hamilton Arts & Letters*, Invisible Publishing, and Wolsak & Wynn for believing in *Ajar* and recommending this project for funding.

Thank you to my family. Thank you, Jacob, for being my world, and thank you to our child, Cosima, new to this world, for such impeccable timing.

ABOUT THE AUTHOR

Margo LaPierre (she/her) is a freelance literary editor and a writer of poetry, fiction, and nonfiction. She has won the *Room* poetry award, the *subTerrain* fiction award, and is the recipient of a SSHRC graduate scholarship. She wrote The Writers' Union of Canada's 2025 guidebook on the author-editor relationship. She has served on *Arc Poetry*'s executive and editorial boards since 2019 and is a member of the poetry collective VII. She holds a Creative Writing MFA from the University of British Columbia and a graduate certificate in publishing from Toronto Metropolitan University. She is a settler living in Ottawa on unceded Algonquin Anishinaabe land. *Ajar* is her second full-length poetry collection.

Printed by Imprimerie Gauvin
Gatineau, Québec